I0616153

Mama's Have Feelings Too:

Parenting with Emotional Intelligence

By Juanita Jones

Mamas Have Feelings Too: Parenting with Emotional Intelligence
Copyright © 2025 by **Juanita Jones**
All rights reserved.

No part of this book may be reproduced, stored in a retrieval system, or transmitted in any form or by any means—electronic, mechanical, photocopying, recording, or otherwise—without prior written permission of the publisher, except for brief quotations used in reviews or critical articles.

For information, permissions, or bulk orders, contact:
Juanita Jones
Email: juanitajonesbooks@gmail.com

Cover design and formatting by Syntax Solutions L.C.

ISBN: 979-8-218-84202-4
First Edition
Publication Date: October 21, 2025

Printed in the United States of America

10 9 8 7 6 5 4 3 2 1

The content of this book is based on the author's personal experiences and reflections. It is intended for educational and inspirational purposes and should not be interpreted as professional medical, psychological, or counseling advice.

Table of Contents

Acknowledgements

This book is a piece of my heart, poured out through words, shaped by life, love, and lessons learned the hard way.

First, to my family: my rock, my reason, my everything. To my children, who have given my life purpose beyond words. To my husband, my partner through decades of military life, deployments, and all the chaos in between. I couldn't have done this without each of you. Thank you for your sacrifices, your patience, and for always holding me down when the weight of the world felt too heavy.

To my sisters and friends, the real ones, you know who you are. The ones who have walked beside me through the highs, the heartbreaks, the late-night talks, and the belly laughs that turned into tears. Your honesty, love, and "pull yourself together" pep talks have carried me through.

To the military spouses who have lived this life with me, I see you. I feel you. The goodbyes, the homecomings, the nights spent praying, the strength we find when we have no other choice, I honor you.

And to you, the reader, thank you for picking up this book, for being open to these words, for walking this journey with me. I hope these pages speak to you, challenge you, and remind you that you're not alone.

With love and gratitude,

Juanita

Introduction: My Story is My Story

My story is my story. I don't know exactly where to begin or how to tell it perfectly, but I know it needs to be told. I'm not going to overthink it I'm just going to talk and let it flow.

Let's start with Miah. When she was born, everything in my life changed. I was just a teenager, 15, maybe 16, trying to figure things out, but becoming a mother at that age wasn't something I ever thought I'd have to prepare for. There were days I didn't think I could do it, nights when I cried because I felt like the world was too heavy. But somehow, I kept going.

There's one moment that always stands out to me. It was the day I walked across that stage at graduation. It felt like everything leading up to that moment had tried to stop me, every obstacle, every doubt, every whispered comment about how I wouldn't make it. I almost didn't graduate. There were times I wanted to give up.

I'll never forget my teachers stepping in to help me. They saw something in me that I couldn't see in myself at the time. They pushed me, encouraged me, and refused to let me quit. I remember the conversations, the support, the way they believed in me even when I didn't.

And then, there I was: walking across the stage, cap and gown on, with Miah waiting for me in the audience. I was proud of myself. Unapologetically proud.

It's not easy to explain what that moment felt like. It was everything: the weight of the struggle, the relief of finishing, the joy of knowing I'd done it not just for me but for my daughter. That's the kind of thing that stays with you.

Looking back, I know the journey wasn't perfect. It was messy, full of mistakes and lessons, but it's my story. And even now, I'm proud of me.

My story is my story, and I own every part of it. The tears, the setbacks, and the moments of doubt shaped me. But so did the victories, the strength I found when I thought I had none left, and the love I poured into my daughter even when I wasn't sure I had enough for myself. Each chapter of my journey has taught me something about resilience, grace, and the power of emotional strength.

Chapter 1: The Turning Point

High school was a whirlwind of emotions, confusion, and life-altering events. I still remember the day my life changed forever, as if it happened yesterday. I was working at TJ Maxx when I started feeling this unrelenting sensation in my stomach. Not like I ate something bad, not cramps, just… strange. It was nothing I'd felt before, and I had no idea what was going on. I couldn't explain it. I told my mom, and she sent my stepdad to come get me. He picked me up from work and took me to Southampton Hospital.

The doctor ran through his routine questions, but one stood out: *"Are you sexually active?"* I didn't even hesitate. "Nope," I lied, straight-faced, with no shame. I'd never been so sure of a lie in my life. "I'm a virgin," I added, putting extra conviction into my words. The doctor just stared at me for a second, and then came the bombshell: *"Well, you're pregnant."*

In that moment, my heart sank to my feet. Pregnant? Me? I couldn't even process it. I sat there stunned, a wave of panic washing over me. My stepdad drove me home in silence, the weight of those words crushing me. When we got home, my mom was sitting on the couch. I didn't know what to say, so I just blurted it out between sobs: "Mom, they said I'm pregnant."

She didn't yell or scream, but the look on her face was enough. It was a disappointment mixed with exhaustion, and that hurt more than any words she could have said. That night, I hugged her tightly, holding her arms down because I didn't know what she might do. But she didn't say much. She just looked at me with sadness that cut deep.

The weeks that followed were some of the hardest in my life. I was pregnant, in high school, and completely unprepared for what was to come. Too much had happened in a short time, and I was terrified. I had to figure it out fast.

By the time school started again in September, I was visibly pregnant. I couldn't hide it anymore. Morning sickness hit me like a freight train. I was constantly running out of classrooms to throw up. Eventually, I had to tell my teachers because I couldn't keep disappearing without an explanation. Some of them were supportive, while others made it clear they thought I was just another stereotype a young Black girl who got pregnant and ruined her life.

Journal and Reflections

What inspired you to start reading this book?

_____

_____

_____

_____

_____

What are your expectations for this journey?

_____

_____

_____

_____

_____

_____

How does the topic relate to your current life experiences?

_____

_____

_____

_____

_____

_____

Chapter 2: My Saving Grace

Then there was Mrs. Mabry, a teacher who saw me as more than my circumstances. She didn't judge me; she helped me. When I ran out of her class to throw up, she would follow me with crackers and tea. She was the one who made me drink unsweetened tea for the first time, insisting it would help. It didn't cure everything, but it made me feel like someone cared. She even called me "Peanut" because I was so small despite being pregnant.

Mrs. Mabry didn't just treat me like a student; she treated me like a human being. She reminded me that I was more than my mistakes and that I could still have a future.

Mr. Burns and Miss Stadler

During my 11th-grade year, my morning sickness got so bad I had to be homeschooled for a while. That's when Mr. Burns and Miss Stadler stepped in. They came to my house. Two teachers who didn't know anything about my life outside of school. They brought baby shower gifts: diapers, a car seat, and a bassinet. They didn't have to do any of that, but they did, and it meant the world to me.

When I returned to school for my senior year, I was failing almost every class. I wasn't focused, I was still trying to live my life, going out and partying like I didn't have a baby on the way. My mom didn't pressure me to be the best; she just wanted me to make it across the finish line. She just wanted me to graduate. But I wasn't even on track for that.

Mr. Burns wasn't having it. He knew I had potential, even when I didn't see it in myself. He gave me one last chance: an essay assignment that could make or break my grade. I don't even remember what the topic was, but I poured my heart into it. When he handed it back to me, he said, "You're going to graduate!"

Graduation Day

Walking across that stage was surreal. My sister, my mom, and my dad were in the audience, holding my baby. As I reached the end of the stage, I walked over to them and picked her up. Holding her in my arms, I realized that everything I had gone through, the pain, the judgment, the struggle, was worth it. I wasn't just walking for me; I was walking for her, too.

That day, I promised myself that no matter what life threw at me, I would keep going. I would be better, not just for me, but for my daughter. And that was the beginning of a new chapter, a chapter where I learned that even when life knocks you down, you can get back up and rewrite your story.

Journal and Reflections

What emotions does this chapter evoke in you?

_____

_____

_____

_____

_____

How do the settings in this chapter align with your personal beliefs?

_____

_____

_____

_____

_____

Can you recall a personal experience related to the topic discussed?

_____

_____

_____

_____

_____

_____

Chapter 3: A Girl from the Hamptons

Yeah, I said it—a girl from the Hamptons, pregnant, not coming from much, not expecting much. People had their assumptions about me, their opinions. I heard it all, the whispers, the judgments. "She's not gonna make it," they said. But you know what? I didn't care. I had my daughter, and I had to make it. For her. For me.

It wasn't pretty, and it wasn't perfect. I messed up sometimes, I'm not gonna lie about that, but I kept moving. That's the thing people don't talk about enough: even when you're struggling, even when you feel like you're at your lowest, you still have to keep going.

And that's why I wanted to write this, why I wanted to say it out loud, unfiltered. Because it's real. I don't care if I mess up while I'm telling it, because this isn't about getting it right; it's about getting it out.

There were days when I felt like the world was on my shoulders. I didn't know how I'd balance it all school, work, being a mom. There were nights when Miah was crying, and I was crying right along with her, thinking, *How am I gonna do this?* But I did it. Not because it was easy, but because I didn't have a choice.

I remember those moments like it was yesterday. No script, no second-guessing. Just me, raw and real. That's how I want this story to feel. Like I'm sitting here with you, just saying what's on my mind.

Because the truth is, I'm proud of myself. And I don't care how many times I mess up in telling this story, it's mine. It's messy, it's hard, and it's beautiful all at the same time.

Chapter 4: East Hampton, Breakups, and Letters from the Past

I grew up in East Hampton, New York. That's home base. I graduated from East Hampton High School, but my life was split between there and Bridgehampton. Every weekend, without fail, I'd be in Bridge at my dad's house. Weekdays were for my mom's house, school, and routine. Weekends? That was a whole different vibe. I'd be in Bridgehampton turning up. No curfew. No bedtime. Just freedom.

East Hampton was cool, but in high school, I wasn't one of the popular girls, not in the school building anyway. But outside of school? Different story. I had people who knew me, loved me, respected me. In school, it was just a tight circle of us, we stuck together. Back then, I didn't have the confidence I carry now.

Looking back, if I had what I have now? Man, I would've been that girl. But I wasn't there yet.

Then life shifted big time. I was in 10th grade when I got pregnant.

It wasn't like I had a whole bunch of partners. But I was young, having fun, thinking love meant forever. I had broken up with my boyfriend, like really broken up. We'd done that back-and-forth breakup dance a few times, but this time it felt final. He left town. I didn't know when he was coming back or if he was coming back.

Not long after, I started messing around with someone else. Not anything serious. Just... it happened. Like I said, we were young and having fun. No one was thinking about consequences. And then... boom.

I'm in the ER, and the doctor looks me in the eye and asks, "Are you sexually active?" And I'm like, "No!" With all the confidence in the world. Like sir, don't play with me. But he looked at me again, dead serious, and asked, "You sure?"

Then he hit me with it: "I don't know how you're not sexually active... because you're pregnant."

Once I processed everything, I told my ex the boyfriend I had broken up with. He was back in town, and when I told him, he was actually happy. Like, *for real* happy. His parents... not so much. But now, looking back, I don't blame them. They had every reason to feel how they felt. Years later, I even apologized to his father, because I believed at the time that his son was the father, and I owed them that grace.

And no, my brain wasn't really thinking about all that before. I mean, we had the "talks" growing up. My mom talked about sex, but it wasn't deep; it wasn't open like that. Not enough for me to think, *If I do this, I could get pregnant.* It just didn't register. I was just living, not thinking about consequences like that.

Time passed, I was still in school, 12th grade by then, and I was a whole mom. I had to have someone watch my baby while I went to class. I was doing it, but it was a lot.

Then one day, I went to check the mail. Normal day. I open the mailbox, and there's this letter from *Willie Jones*. Now, I hadn't seen or heard from Willie in *years*. We grew up together. Our dads were best friends. Every time my dad came down to Florida for Christmas, spring break, and summer. He'd pick me up and take me to hang out with his best friend's family. That's how I'd always see Willie.

But when our dads weren't involved, we didn't really see each other. Our moms weren't that close, and we lived in different places, so it was just those visits. But now here I was, living in East Hampton again, raising my baby, and I get this letter out the blue.

Turns out, Willie had asked about me. My dad didn't give him my number. This was back before everybody had cell phones, but he gave him my mailing address. So, Willie, who was in the military, wrote me. A whole page and a half, just catching me up, letting me know where he was, giving me his number.

I called him.

That first call? We picked up like we never left off. Like time hadn't passed. It was easy. Familiar. It felt like we'd just been paused, not apart. After that, we didn't stop talking. Not once.

And that's where the next chapter starts with a letter in the mail, a phone call, and a connection that went deeper than we ever expected.

Chapter 5: Breaking the Silence

I didn't grow up in a house where kids had a voice. Hell, I grew up in a house where asking a question could get you in trouble. It was " do as I say and not as I do." Period. No explanations. No conversations. No space for curiosity. And I learned quickly that if I wanted to know anything, I had to keep my mouth shut and just listen.

So, I listened. I heard everything.
Conversations I wasn't supposed to hear. Secrets adults thought I was too young to understand. But I understood. I just wasn't allowed to ask about it. And the more I listened, the more I realized this ain't how I want to raise my kids.
I knew what it felt like to be a child full of questions but too scared to ask them. I remember that frustration, that helplessness, that

deep need to understand, but knowing if I dared speak up, I'd be shut down. I carried that with me, and when I had my own kids, I made a choice. A promise. My children would never feel like they had to swallow their words just to keep the peace.

So, I did the opposite. I gave them freedom. The freedom to ask. The freedom to speak. The freedom to tell me when I'm wrong, even when it stings. And trust me, sometimes it stings like hell. Because when you give your kids the space to tell their truth, that means they can call you out, too. And they will.

But that's what real love looks like. That's what real honesty looks like. I didn't want to be the kind of mother who only told the good parts of my story. I wanted to be the mother who showed my kids the whole picture the good, the bad, and the ugly. Because if I want them to be honest with me, I have to be honest with them.

 Journal and Reflections

What are some things you weren't allowed to ask about as a child? How did that shape the way you communicate today?

_____

_____

_____

_____

_____

_____

If you have kids (or plan to), how do you want to approach conversations differently than how you were raised?

_____

_____

_____

_____

What fears do you have about giving your children the freedom to speak their minds?

_____

_____

_____

_____

_____

_____

Chapter 6: The First Conversation

It was the first time I realized just how deeply my child's feelings mattered. My oldest came to me, just four years old at the time, and said something that stopped me in my tracks: "Mom, Daddy doesn't love me. He only loves Liyah."

She called him "Daddy," even though he was her stepfather. Those words hit me like a ton of bricks. She wasn't asking for attention or trying to stir things up this was her truth, and at only four years old, she felt brave enough to tell me. That was her first deep conversation, and it was my wake-up call.

I remember thinking, *How does a child so young even feel this way? What has she seen or felt to make her believe that love is uneven in our home?* It wasn't her birthday or any special occasion, just a regular day. But for her, this was something she needed to let out, and I had to listen.

Her words forced me to stop and pay attention not just to what she was saying, but to everything. I started questioning how our family dynamics might be affecting her, and whether I was creating a space where she felt truly safe and heard.

I shared this moment with my husband, and he was taken aback too. He admitted he hadn't realized how his actions, even unintentionally, might be making her feel less loved. To his credit, he took it seriously. That moment shifted things for us as a family it wasn't about assigning blame but about understanding how we could do better.

Why This Matters

That conversation with my daughter was more than just a moment; it was a lesson in the power of communication between parents and children. It taught me that even at four years old, kids are deeply perceptive. They pick up on things we might not even notice ourselves.

This chapter is for every parent who wants to create that bond, a bond where their child knows they can come to them with anything, no matter how small or big. It's about breaking cycles of silence and fear, especially for those little girls who might be too scared to go to their mothers with their pain or questions.

When my daughter came to me, it wasn't just about her. It was about creating a legacy where she and every child that I hope this book reaches feels safe enough to speak their truth.

Chapter 7: A Real Conversation Between Mother and Daughters

Writing this chapter has been healing for me, too, but through my journey with my daughters, I've realized that I can break that cycle. I can be the mother she needs and, in doing so, heal the little girl inside of me who once felt lost and unheard.

This chapter is for you, the reader, too. Whether you're a parent, a daughter, or someone still healing from childhood wounds, let this story remind you that it's never too late to create spaces of love and understanding.

It started in the group chat. Not from me but between my daughters. And like many family dynamics, it was short, loaded, and ripe with tension.

Miah, my oldest, was planning a small gathering with friends. She wanted it to be light, fun just a space to breathe after a stressful week. She had the whole night planned. She was inviting all her people, making sure the vibe was right, and ensuring everybody could come out and enjoy themselves. But as always, one little thing had to stir up drama before the night even started.

"I know you invited everybody," her younger sister Liyah texted her, "but if he's coming, I might just stay home."

Just like that, the mood shifted.

Miah called me, voice tight with frustration. "Why does she have to do this every time?" she asked. "I'm not trying to get in the middle of it, but now I feel like I have to choose."

I could hear the weight in her voice. Not just the annoyance, but something deeper. The feeling of being caught between peacekeeping and self-respect.

In the past, I might have rushed to fix it. I might have told her to cancel the whole thing or call Liyah and make her talk it out right then and there. But I've learned slowly, sometimes painfully, that emotional intelligence isn't about rushing toward resolution. It's about sitting in discomfort long enough to understand where it's coming from.

"Maybe it's not even about him," I said gently. "Maybe there's something underneath. Something between you two that hasn't been said."

We sat in silence for a few seconds.
She sighed. "It always feels like I have to be the one to hold everything together."

There it was. Not just a sister-to-sister conflict but a familiar burden. One I knew too well.

"Miah, it's okay to want peace," I told her. "But you don't have to sacrifice clarity for it. You're allowed to ask for honesty. To ask people to show up whole or not at all."

Liyah enters the chat. "Yo, I know you inviting everybody, but I ain't really tryna be around him like that. So, if he coming, I might just stay home."

Miah sighed. "Liyah, what you mean? We all cool. What's the issue now?"

Liyah paused for a second. "It ain't even like that, Miah. I told you before, I don't really mess with him like that. It's just... I don't like being around him, and I don't need to explain myself every time."

Miah wasn't one to force nobody into uncomfortable situations, but something in Liyah's voice wasn't sitting right with her. "Sis, you my sister, so of course, if you tell me you don't want somebody there, I'ma respect that. But I also need to know why. Because from where I stand, it sound like you still got some type of feelings you don't wanna admit."

Liyah scoffed. "Man, what? Miah, stop. It ain't that."

"Then what is it?" Miah pressed. "Because if it's just about that little thing y'all had before, that ain't no reason for all this energy."

Liyah exhaled hard. "Look, it ain't even about him like that. I just feel some type of way because every time we all in the same space, he act like we cool, but I know what it was. And I don't need to be around that energy."

Miah nodded, understanding but also sensing something deeper. "So if you over it, why he still got power over your mood like that? If it's nothing, it should be nothing, right? But the way you talking, it sound like it's still something."

Liyah was silent for a moment. "I don't know, man. Maybe I just don't trust myself around him. Maybe it's the history, maybe it's the way he move, I don't know. I just don't like it."

"Then say that," Miah said. "But don't make it seem like it's about me not respecting your boundaries. Because I always do. I just wanna make sure you being real with yourself."

Liyah smirked. "Alright, therapist Miah. You got me. Maybe I need to figure some things out. But tonight, I still ain't tryna be around him."

Miah laughed. "Say less, sis. He ain't coming. But next time, let's have a real convo before it get to this point."

Liyah nodded. "Bet. I appreciate you."

I hung, shaking her head. This was what it meant to have emotional intelligence being able to read between the lines, respect boundaries, but also hold the people you love accountable for their own feelings.

That night wasn't just about a party. It was about helping both my daughter's to name their boundaries. Helping them realize that emotional intelligence isn't just about being understanding, it's about being honest. It's about recognizing when someone else's discomfort is spilling into your space and having the courage to lovingly call it out.

Miah didn't cancel the gathering. She didn't send a dramatic group text. She reached out to her sister directly. Not with anger but with curiosity. And what followed wasn't a perfect resolution, but it was a beginning. A thread of real communication that hadn't been there before.

When I hung up the phone, I felt proud not just of Liyah and Miah, but of myself.

Because once upon a time, I didn't know how to allow these conversations. I avoided hard topics. I mistook silence for safety. But here I am now, guiding my daughters through the very emotional landscapes I used to fear.

This is what growth looks like not loud, not flashy. Just a mother and daughters, learning to listen a little deeper. Speak a little braver. Love a little better.

Journal and Reflections

When was the last time you avoided a hard conversation to keep the peace? What did it cost you emotionally or relationally?

_____

_____

_____

_____

_____

Think of a recent moment when someone's reaction confused or frustrated you. What might have been going on beneath the surface—for them and for you?

_____

_____

_____

_____

In your relationships, do you often feel like the "peacekeeper"? Where did you learn that role, and how does it serve (or burden) you?

_____

_____

_____

_____

_____

What does emotional intelligence mean to you today? How has your understanding of it changed over time?

_____

_____

_____

_____

_____

_____

Imagine you're guiding someone younger—your child, niece, mentee—through a tough emotional moment. What would you say to help them unpack their feelings with honesty and care?

_____

_____

_____

_____

_____

_____

Write about a time you were proud of yourself for showing emotional maturity. What did that moment teach you?

_____

_____

_____

_____

_____

Chapter 8: Be My Friend

There comes a time when my kids come to me, and they talk to me. They tell me about myself, and sometimes, they come at me hard. But I feel like when we reach that level, we take another step up. I feel it because at one point, they wouldn't talk to me. At one point, they wouldn't even try. So, for them to come to me now, even if it feels like they're coming for me, it's a breakthrough.

But let me make this clear if you're just trying to hurt my feelings, that's not going to work. If you're just coming at me to come at me, then no. But if you're telling me about myself because I need to hear it, then I have to listen. I have to take that in and really sit with it. Because if my kids are telling me something is bothering them, I need to respect that.

See, I always tell them, "Tell me about myself." Because I need that honesty. They need to know they can speak freely with me without fear. There are kids out there who can't go to their moms and say what's on their hearts. I don't want that for mine. I don't want them to feel like they have to hold back because I'll react poorly. I had to come to them first and say, "Tell me the truth. Don't walk on eggshells around me. If I'm messing up, let me know."

I had a conversation with Miah, and she said something that hit me deep. She said, "Mama, I feel like you're above that." And I understood exactly what she meant. It wasn't about the situation; it was about what she saw in me, what she knew I deserved. And at that moment, I had to take that in. Because that was her looking out for me, not just as my daughter, but as my friend. That's when I knew we had reached a different kind of understanding.

I need my kids to talk to me, not sugarcoat things. I tell them all the time don't water it down, don't try to spare my feelings. Talk to me like a person, not just your mama. Because if we're not real with each other, what's the point? They may not always have the emotional intelligence yet to say things the right way, but that's okay. We'll figure it out together.

I had to learn that there are times when they need their mother, and times when they need their friend. And sometimes, I need my friend too. I need my kids to step up and say, "Mama, let me tell you something," without fear. That's respect. That's trust. That's love.

I don't always know everything, and I'm not afraid to admit that. When you're young, you think your parents are superheroes, that they have it all figured out. But I let my kids see every side of me the mother, the human, the person who gets mad, who cries, who loves hard. Because I don't ever want them to be afraid to be themselves with me.

At the end of the day, my kids are my ride-or-die. They came from me, and no matter what, we will always find our way back to each other. We may fight, we may argue, we may need space but we will always be solid. Because they know I will always listen, and I know they will always tell me the truth. And that's all I could ever ask for.

Chapter 9: The Line Between

There's a thin line between being your kid's parent and being their friend, and I'll be honest, I cross it more than I probably should. Not 'cause I'm out here trying to be the "cool mom" or scared to lay down the law. Nah. It's deeper than that. I cross that line because I *remember* what it felt like to be a kid who wasn't allowed to ask "why." To question. To feel. To *be*. I grew up in a house where silence was safer than honesty, where being quiet was mistaken for being respectful, and where kids were told, *"Because I said so,"* like that was enough.

That's not the world I wanted for my babies. I want them to speak up, challenge stuff, say what's on their minds even when it makes me uncomfortable. And for the most part? They do. Oh, they *do*. They talk freely in this house, sometimes too freely, if I'm being real.

Sometimes they hit me with things that stop me in my tracks, make me catch my breath and question everything I thought I was doing right.

Like when my daughter said something slick about my wifely duties to my husband, noting needing to "submit" to my husband, something she probably picked up on a podcast or maybe from one of *my* old rants, I don't even know. One day I was venting to my daughter, just letting it all out, and she hit me with, "So what you can't be happy unless you have money?" And in that moment, I realized s*he* tied success to the same belief I've spent years trying to unlearn—that success and happiness are only real if your bank account says so. And in that moment? Whew. I had to sit with it. I had to ask myself: in all this openness, this transparency I thought was so powerful... had I gone too far? Was I helping them find their truth—or just dumping mine on them?

See, raising emotionally intelligent kids ain't just about letting them talk. It's about knowing *how* to respond. Knowing when to speak and when to shut up and let them process. And I'll admit, sometimes I overshare. Sometimes I forget they're still learning how to hold their own weight, and I hand them mine too. That's not fair. That's not their job.

But still, I don't regret creating a home where feelings are allowed to breathe. Where nobody gets told "man up" or "stop crying" or "get over it." My kids feel things deeply, they speak up for themselves, they hold their ground. And even when they come at me sideways, I see it: I'm raising kids who *know themselves*. And that matters more to me than them keeping quiet to keep the peace.

One night, after a particularly tough conversation with my oldest, I sat on the edge of my bed and cried. Not because I was hurt by what she said, but because I saw myself in her. The fire, the passion, the questions. But I also saw my fears staring back at me fears I hadn't meant to pass on. That moment was heavy, but it was necessary. It reminded me that parenting isn't about perfection. It's about presence.

There's no manual for this. No blueprint. Just love, patience, and a whole lotta self-awareness. Some days I get it right. Other days? Not so much. But every day, I show up. I listen. I apologize when I need to. I let them see me be human, so they know it's okay to be human too.

Parenting ain't no straight line. It's messy. It's a dance between letting them grow and not letting them get crushed under the stuff we still haven't healed from. And I'm still learning every damn day. But one thing I know for sure? My kids will never wonder if their voice matters. Not in this house. Not with this mama. They'll know they can speak, they'll know they'll be heard, and they'll never have to shrink just to survive.

Chapter 10: A Real Conversation Between Mother and Son

It's funny how you can learn the most about your kids when you're not even trying. I wasn't snooping. I wasn't eavesdropping. I was just in the house, moving through the day like always, and I overheard my son and his friends talking while they were visiting. The conversation was easy to miss, teenage boys being teenage boys, but something caught my attention.

One of them read a message out loud. It was from a girl. And I don't know everything that was said, but I caught enough to know that the message had a certain… tone. It was a little too grown. The kind of thing that makes you, as a mom, pause. It didn't sit right with me.

I didn't react right away. I didn't call him out in front of his friends that's never the move. But I watched his face. And that's what told me everything I needed to know. He didn't laugh like the others. He didn't chime in. His body went stiff, his eyes went quiet. He wasn't about to confirm or deny anything. He just shut down.

That's when I knew: he wasn't ready to talk about it. Not there. Not like that.

So, I waited.

Later that day, it was just him and me. We were in the car just riding. And if you know anything about car rides, you know they're magic. Something about being side by side instead of face to face makes things easier. No pressure. No spotlight. Just space. He couldn't go anywhere. I couldn't go anywhere. So, I brought it up. Gently. "Hey," I said, "what was that conversation earlier about that girl?"

He didn't say much at first. Just kind of shrugged, then said, "Yeah… she said some things." I nodded. "Okay. And how did that make you feel?" Now, let me tell you something, when I asked him that, he didn't jump in with a deep answer. He looked away. Gave a little smirk. Said nothing.

I could tell he didn't want to say the wrong thing. Maybe he thought I'd be mad. Maybe he didn't know how to explain it. But I knew *I knew* as a teenage boy, getting a message like that was going to stir something up.

So, before he could even say it, I reassured him. I said, "Whatever you felt, it's okay. I'm not here to judge. You're human. I'm human. What you feel doesn't make you bad or wrong. It just makes you real."

That's when he let out a breath. And with a little smirk, he said, "Honestly, it made me feel good."
I smiled. "That's okay."

That moment? That was everything. Because it wasn't about the message. It wasn't about the girl. It was about giving him a safe space to say what he was feeling and to know that he wouldn't be punished for it. I told him, "Your feelings are valid. They don't always make you right, and they don't always mean you should act on them, but they are real. And the more honest you are about them, the more you'll understand yourself. Some people run from their feelings. But around here, we *feel* our feelings. That's how we grow."

That conversation turned into a lesson for both of us. Him, learning that emotions aren't something to be ashamed of. Me, learning that creating space for our kids to feel safe with their emotions matters more than any lecture I could give.

I know a lot of people who are uncomfortable with emotions. They were raised to push feelings down, toughen up, stay quiet. But I want more for my kids. I want them to grow up emotionally aware, able to name what they feel and express it with honesty. Emotional intelligence isn't soft it's powerful.

So yeah, it was just a car ride. Just a little chat. But it was a big deal. Because that day, my son learned that he could be real with me. That he could say something that felt a little messy, and I'd still hear him out with love, not judgment.

And I hope he carries that with him. I hope all my kids do.

Because feelings? They're meant to be felt.

Chapter 11: The Balance Between Mother and Friend

Being open with my kids came naturally to me, but I had to learn how to balance it. While I wanted them to talk to me like a friend, I also had to remind them that I was still their mother. That's a tricky line to walk.

When you're raising kids, you want them to trust you. You want them to know they can come to you with anything. But at the same time, you have to maintain authority. You have to be able to guide them, teach them, and discipline them when needed. Sometimes, I felt like I was blurring that line too much.

One conversation with my daughter really made me reflect on this. I was venting about something small something as simple as my frustration with turning my husband's socks right-side out before washing them. And my daughter, listening to me, responded with, "Isn't that what a wife is supposed to do?"

That moment hit me hard. To her, it was just a normal part of life, something expected of me as a wife. But to me, it was deeper than that. It wasn't just about socks it was about fairness, effort, and expectations in a relationship. And I had to explain that to her.

There were other moments too, when I realized my transparency was giving them a skewed perspective. When I talked about struggles money, relationships, life in general I thought I was teaching them lessons, giving them insight so they wouldn't have to learn the hard way. But in reality, sometimes all they saw was the struggle. They saw the hard parts, the frustrations, the moments of doubt, and they started wondering if life was just a series of problems to be solved.

That's when I had to step back. I had to remember that being open didn't mean overwhelming them. That being real didn't mean only sharing the struggles. I had to show them the joys too—the wins, the moments of ease, the simple happiness in everyday life.

Because if all they heard was hardship, then what was I really teaching them?

Parenting isn't about being perfect. It's about growing, learning, and adjusting. It's about recognizing when you need to shift and doing the work to make it right. And that's exactly what I did. I learned that I could be both a mother and a friend. I could listen, I could guide, and I could love them in a way that made them feel free while still giving them the structure they needed.

Because at the end of the day, that's what being a mother is really about finding the balance and making sure your kids feel safe enough to be exactly who they are.

Chapter 12: Respect Over Fear: Building Strong Parent-Child Relationships

Let me just start by saying: parenting ain't easy, and it definitely doesn't come with a manual. We learn as we go, sometimes messing up, sometimes getting it right, but always trying. One of the biggest lessons I've learned on this ride is that fear might get quick results, but it won't get you real connection with your kids. Respect will, every time.

I grew up in a house where you didn't talk back, you didn't question, and you definitely didn't show too many emotions. If you stepped out of line, you felt it. The belt, the look, the silence, whatever it was, you knew fear. And yeah, I listened. But not because I understood. I followed the rules because I didn't want the smoke, not because I agreed or felt respected.

When I became a mom, I had to really sit with that. Did I want my kids to flinch when I raised my voice? Or did I want them to trust me enough to come talk to me when life got messy? I chose the second one. But let me tell you, it's a daily choice, and it's not always easy.

I'm not saying my kids don't get on my nerves sometimes or that I don't lose it. I'm human. But I try not to lead with fear. Because fear might keep them in line for now, but respect? Respect will stick with them for life.

Let's talk about what that looks like.

Why Fear Falls Short. I know some of us were raised to believe that spanking equals discipline. That if a kid ain't scared of you, they're gonna run wild. But here's the thing fear teaches kids to hide, to lie, to shrink. They'll follow rules, but they won't understand why. And worse, they won't come to you when it really matters because they don't feel safe.

I've seen it in real life. I've been that kid, afraid to tell my parents when I messed up or needed help. And I don't want that for my babies. I want them to know that even if they screw up, they can come to me.

Building Respect Starts With Us. Respect in parenting isn't about letting kids do whatever they want. It's about showing up with consistency, communication, and love. Here's what that looks like in my house:

1. **Say It More Than Once** Kids don't get it the first time. Or the second. Sometimes you gotta repeat yourself over and over before it clicks. But that's parenting. We plant seeds and water them, even when we don't see growth right away.

2. **Lead by Example** If I want my kids to be respectful, I have to show them what that looks like. That means checking my own tone, listening to them, and handling stress in a way I'd want them to mirror.

3. **Break It Down** When they mess up, I don't just say, "Because I said so." I explain why something isn't okay and what the impact is. They need to understand the *why* behind the rule.

4. **Let Them Talk** Even when it's uncomfortable. Even when I don't

agree. My kids know they can come to me and speak their minds. That doesn't mean I always say yes, but it means they're heard.

5. **Correct with Care** Discipline should teach, not tear down. I want my kids to leave a conversation feeling like they're still loved, not like they're a disappointment.

Breaking Old Cycles This parenting style ain't what I saw growing up. I had to unlearn a lot. But when I see my kids express themselves without fear, or tell me the truth even when it's hard, I know I'm doing something right.

I remember once, I was venting about money stressed, overwhelmed and my daughter looked at me and said, "So you can't be happy unless you have money?" Whew. That hit different. I realized right then that some of the stuff I thought I was shielding them from, they were still absorbing. The very thing I was trying to escape the pressure to tic joy to struggle or success to income was showing up in their words. That made me pause and reflect. Our kids are watching, even when we think they're not.

The Bigger Picture At the end of the day, I want my children to grow into adults who know how to express themselves, make decisions with integrity, and treat people with kindness not because they fear the consequences, but because they understand the value of doing what's right.

This isn't about being perfect. It's about being present, being open, and being willing to grow alongside our kids. Respect over fear, every time.

And if no one told you today: You're doing better than you think.

Keep going, mama.

Chapter 13: The Freedom to Speak
Part I

Giving my kids freedom wasn't just about letting them talk, it was about truly listening. And let me tell you, listening ain't always easy.

When you let your kids be honest with you, that means sometimes they're going to say things you don't want to hear. They're going to tell you when you've hurt them, when you've fallen short, when you've let them down. And that's hard. It's hard as hell to sit there and hear your child say, "Mom, when you did that, it hurt me."

My first instinct? Defend myself. Explain. Make excuses. But I had to check myself. If I wanted my kids to trust me enough to speak their truth, I had to be strong enough to take it. No matter how uncomfortable it made me.

And it's not just about parenting. This is about relationships in general. If you care about somebody, whether it's your child, your partner, or your best friend, you gotta be willing to hear them out. If someone tells you that something you did made them feel bad, you don't get to decide how they feel. You don't get to shut them down because it makes you uncomfortable. You have to be real enough to take accountability.

The way I see it, my kids are human just like me. They have emotions just like me. And if I don't give them the space to express those emotions, then what kind of mother am I? What kind of example am I setting?

Freedom is freedom. It doesn't come with conditions. If I give my kids the freedom to talk, that means they get to tell the truth whether I like it or not. And as much as it challenges me, it also makes me better. It forces me to grow. It makes me check myself. Because at the end of the day, I don't just want my kids to love me I want them to trust me.

 Journal and Reflections

When was the last time someone called you out on something? How did you react?

_____

_____

_____

_____

_____

_____

How do you usually respond to criticism? Do you shut down, get defensive, or reflect?

_____

_____

_____

_____

_____

_____

What's one thing your child (or someone close to you) has told you that forced you to check yourself?

_____

_____

_____

_____

_____

How can you create a space where your loved ones feel safe to tell you the truth?

_____

_____

_____

_____

_____

_____

Chapter 14: Raising Truth Speakers

I didn't grow up in a house where kids had a say. You spoke when spoken to, and you damn sure didn't question authority especially not a parent. I remember watching grown folks say things that didn't add up, but my job was to nod and keep it moving. If I had a thought that contradicted theirs, I swallowed it. If I felt disrespected, I dealt with it. That's just how it was.

Now, here I am, 41 years old, a mother of three, and I'm raising my kids in a way that would've had me labeled as "disrespectful" when I was their age. In my house, my kids can challenge me not to be rude, but to be real. If something doesn't make sense to them, they can ask questions. If they're hurt, they can say so. If I mess up, they can call me out. And let me tell you, it ain't always easy.

Sometimes, I hear my kids say things that make me pause, make me uncomfortable, make me rethink everything I thought I knew about parenting. Like when my oldest told me, "Ma, sometimes you don't listen. You hear me, but you don't really listen." Whew. That hit.

But here's the thing I want them to be whole. I want them to be confident in their voices. I don't want them walking into adulthood still trying to find the courage to say what they mean because they were shut down as kids. I don't want them thinking respect is the same as silence.

I'm breaking cycles, but breaking ain't easy. There are moments I feel like I'm doing too much, giving them too much space, making them too comfortable. Then I remind myself raising kids who know how to speak their truth is not a mistake; it's a mission.

 Journal and Reflections

What messages did you receive about speaking up when you were a child? How has that shaped the way you express yourself now?

_____

_____

_____

_____

_____

_____

Have you ever felt silenced by authority figures in your life? How did that experience impact you?

_____

_____

_____

_____

What are some things you've wanted to say but held back because you were taught it was "disrespectful"?

_____

_____

_____

_____

_____

If you're a parent or want to be one someday, how do you want your children to experience communication in your home?

_____

_____

_____

_____

_____

_____

What does respect mean to you? Is it about obedience, understanding, or something else?

_____

_____

_____

_____

_____

_____

How do you react when someone challenges your perspective? Do you shut down, defend yourself, or stay open to the conversation?

_____

_____

_____

_____

_____

What's one thing you can start doing today to create space for honest conversations in your relationships?

_____

_____

_____

_____

_____

If your younger self could speak freely without fear, what would they say to the adults in their life?

_____

_____

_____

_____

_____

Raising truth speakers isn't just about them—it's about me too. It's about unlearning, relearning, and making sure the cycle of silence ends with me.

Chapter 15: The Freedom to Speak
Part II

Motherhood was never about following a script for me. It wasn't about pretending everything was fine or keeping quiet about the hard stuff. From the start, I wanted to give my kids what I never had the freedom to speak, to ask questions, to feel heard. Growing up, I often felt like my words didn't matter, like I was just supposed to be seen and not heard. That silence stuck with me. So, when I had kids, I knew I had to do things differently.

I didn't have a rigid plan, nor did I sit down one day and decide, "This is how I'm going to raise my kids." But as I watched them grow and navigate the world around them, I realized they had questions. It didn't matter whether those questions were small or big, I knew they needed answers. And I wanted to be the one giving them those answers, not the world, not their friends, not strangers.

At some point, I made a conscious decision: My kids would always have the space to talk to me. They wouldn't have to hold things in like I did. Their father played a big role in this too, showing them that it was okay to express themselves. But as their mother, I made sure they knew they could say what they needed to say to me, without fear of judgment or punishment.

Because freedom in a family isn't just about letting kids do what they want, it's about creating an environment where they feel safe enough to be themselves and speak their truth. And when they talked to me, when they really opened up, it made me feel good. Not just as a mother, but as a person. It meant I had done something right.

Journal and Reflections

How has this book impacted you?

_____

_____

_____

_____

_____

What lasting lessons will you carry forward?

_____

_____

_____

_____

_____

What would you tell someone else about this book and its influence on you?

_____

_____

_____

_____

_____

About the Author

Juanita Jones is a proud wife, mother, and first-time author who believes laughter, love, and good vibes make life beautiful. Born in Florida and raised in New York, she now calls Georgia home, where she enjoys karaoke nights, family time, and the company of her two Yorkies, Chase and Skye—named after her favorite Paw Patrol pups.

With an associate degree in Early Childhood Education, Juanita has spent her life nurturing others while learning the importance of nurturing herself. Married at eighteen and now celebrating twenty-three years of marriage, she is the mother of three children, ages sixteen, nineteen, and twenty-six.

In *Mamas Have Feelings Too: Parenting with Emotional Intelligence*, Juanita writes from the heart as a normal woman and mom who simply wanted to share what she's learned about motherhood, balance, and emotional growth. At forty-one, she continues to live with gratitude, humor, and faith, hoping to remind every mama that it's okay to feel, heal, and enjoy the journey.

www.ingramcontent.com/pod-product-compliance
Lightning Source LLC
Chambersburg PA
CBHW061707120626
46550CB00003B/1131